Published by Anglican House Publishers, Inc. serving the Anglican Church in North America and the Body of Christ. You may contact us at http://www.ahpub.org

Edited and designed by Ron Speers using *Optima* font. Printed in the United States.

Anglican House
Publishers

ISBN 978-1-62407-511-7

The Way Forward

Nurturing New Believers

The *Christian Foundations* Course

Michael Green

Anglican House
Publishers

"In *The Way Forward* Michael Green brings to bear on the topic of discipleship the fruits of his long and distinguished ministry experience in the field of evangelism. For those just starting the process of discipleship – either as a leader or a beginning disciple – I give my most hearty recommendation to *The Way Forward.* In a word, it is *elegant.* It is beautiful in its effectiveness and simplicity, making it both doable and reproducible."

Todd Hunter
Anglican Bishop, Author and Professor
Rector, Holy Trinity Church, Costa Mesa, CA

"New-born Christians urgently need the milk of God's word to help them grow strong in the faith. This book equips the church to provide exactly that. Michael Green distils a lifetime of experience in evangelism and disciple-making into this tried and tested method that gives Christian leaders the joy of helping new believers take their first steps. It is a wonderful resource for local churches and para-church organizations. I hope it will be widely used to raise up new Christians, and new leaders, for the life of the church today."

The Very Rev Dr Justyn Terry
Dean and President, Trinity School For Ministry

"*The Way Forward*" is both practical and timely. Michael Green shares his method – his life's learning really – for taking new believers into Bible reading and small group fellowship. The book outlines a way to take new converts into basic discipleship. What is offered here can be employed in any circumstance, by any congregation, to ground those newly come to Christ, in behaviors and relationships that will sustain them beyond those early days."

Archbishop Bob Duncan
Anglican Church in North America

"Michael has given us a thoughtful, practical and needed tool with *The Way Forward*. It is thorough and easy to use for small groups. It's theologically sound and leaves room for the Holy Spirit to work. This will be a huge help for new believers."

The Rev Dr John Yates
Rector, The Falls Church Anglican

"Michael Green has earned the right to call us out. We have too often failed to help the new or young follower of Christ to start the journey of faith well. It should not be a surprise that without intentional support and skillful guidance, the new or young believer will not advance far and travel safely. So, Michael Green takes us to Acts 2 to see how the early Christians got it right. And he then shows us a six-session game plan so we can successfully do the same today. He offers sound and proven advice to any who will assume responsibility to nurture and make a lasting impact on the new and young believer. Leaders in every church: Get copies of *The Way Forward* into the hands of men and women – and coach them to implement this plan. You need to make room for this in your toolbox of essential resources."

Don Willett, PhD
Author and Founder of Stages of Faith Ministries

INTRODUCTION

This is a short, simple, introductory course to the Christian life for those who have just professed faith or are very seriously considering it. This makes it different from *Christianity Explored* (which is a sequential study of St. Mark) or *Alpha* which (though a topical course like this) is designed for those who are not yet Christians and who need to have a longer approach to the faith.

In recent years churches have depended on these fairly lengthy courses for much of their evangelistic outreach, and many of the members of these groups become Christians by the end of the course. Their whole approach is so valuable because many today start so far behind the start line about Christianity that an immediate challenge would be inappropriate because an extended period of exploring the faith is needed. That I entirely understand, and I am most enthusiastic for all that *Alpha* and *Christianity Explored* continue to achieve in bringing people to Christ.

But the idea seems to be prevalent in Christian circles today that *proclamation evangelism* (preaching evangelistically for decision) is no longer effective. That is not the case. I have seen a great many people come to trust Christ after a sermon, and in that case they absolutely need something to sustain them and to help them to grow. Unfortunately there is not a great deal available. And although I make no great claims for this course – the *Christian Foundations* course – I know from long experience that it is very effective. It has not been published before, but I have often been asked for it, and am now somewhat belatedly making it available. It is designed for those who would like to lead or help lead a study group of new Christians. You will find something of the philosophy of the course in the first three chapters, followed by the material for each of six evening sessions, as well as some further information in three Supplements at the end.

The Christian Foundations course has been used in four continents, and has proved a very effective way of getting new "Babes in Christ" started successfully. It depends a good deal on the commitment and care of the leaders, and it does not attempt to clone them or constrict them by producing talks for them to copy for use each night, but instead offers healthy material, some of which should be included in the leaders' talks, though expressed in his or her own way. The *Christian Foundations* course is designed to help the participants to discover the power and the joy of the scriptures, to find the attractiveness of Christian fellowship, to get them launched in prayer, able to cope with the temptations that will surely come their way, and prepare them for a life of Christian witness and service.

I hope it will be a real help, especially for those who preach for decision and are looking for some suitable material for the follow-up.

Michael Green

Christmas 2012

ONE

The Great Need

I have been privileged to lead evangelistic missions in all of the five continents during my long life, and it is an unfailing joy and privilege to see men and women entrusting their lives to Jesus Christ. But I am not at all convinced of the quality and effectiveness of the after-care offered to those who profess their faith. It is usually very weak and unsystematic, if it is even attempted at all.

I'm afraid Many evangelists seem content to see hands raised or some other mode of response, at the end of their address, and then to go away counting these as conversions. But that may well not be the case. Those concerned may at best have made a hesitant profession of faith that needs to be carefully nourished. Sadly, this care is often lacking.

Why?

In church circles, the prevalent idea seems to be that new believers can slot easily into the regular worship of the church. However, church culture is massively different from what most of them have been reared in all their lives. The singing of hymns is alien to most red-blooded males. The idea that one person up front should speak uninterrupted for up to twenty minutes is repellent to those used to the speedy interaction of *Facebook* or *Twitter.*

And So-called "fellowship time" afterwards, with weak tea served in green cups and saucers (British) or coffee in Styrofoam cups (American) is not the easy fellowship of the pub or an American sports bar. Clearly, your new believers are going to need some help if they are to going to be able to adjust to the fresh world of being in Christ!

If that is the case in the churches, the need is just as critical in the universities. Most Christian Unions (British) or Christian organizations in American colleges and universities constitute a very small proportion of the university population. Their number are looked down on by the many who regarded them as rather pathetic. They do not get drunk or fornicate and seem to lead grey and lacklustre lives. Worse, they tend, like most small minority groups to be, well, pretty inwardly-looking, fundamentalist in their convictions, and unable to relate easily to those who are not of their persuasion. These have their own inherited patterns of behavior that seem very strange to the rest of the student body. And yet, when a fellow student comes to a Christian commitment, these are the people who are expected to take care of him or her! "Oh, let the students handle the follow-up," seems to be the attitude in the afterglow of many a campus mission. And of course the students mostly haven't a clue how to set about this *it.*

Amazingly, some of the new believers at the crusade or church or on campus manage to survive, and to make the massive jump to Bible studies, daily devotions, prayer meetings and the rest. But a great many fall by the wayside. It is obvious that we are not very good at helping new believers to make the transition to this massively different life on which they've embarked.

Amazing too is the real shortage of materials that can be used to address the critical need of nurturing a new believer. Partly this may be due to the emphasis in recent decades on what one might call *process evangelism,* where people are invited to join an extended course designed for enquirers, such as *Alpha* or *Christianity Explored* or an inquirers class at your church. *Proclamation evangelism,* i.e., preaching for decision, has fallen into disuse. Church people seem to think that nobody comes to God after hearing the gospel for the first time.

But they *do*!

Only last night I was speaking during a Christmas production in of all places a nightclub. *Twelve* people responded then and there to the challenge to invite Christ into their lives. People like that need a short course of instruction that will help them to find their Christian sea legs before being thrown helter-skelter into an alien world of church services and perhaps even more alien world of church culture.

The First Christians Got It Right

At all events, the first Christians did not make this mistake of failing to provide adequate nurture for those babes who had only just then come to faith. Jesus commissioned his friends to go and make disciples of all nations, not simply to call for decisions. Acts 2 gives us an insight about how they went about it. First, they carefully noted who the new converts were (Acts 2:41). No doubt names were taken, the ancient equivalent of contact information was collected, and friendly faces greeted them. People like to be recognised and remembered. Then they baptised them (Acts 2:41).

These new believers *needed* to undergo the rite of initiation which Jesus himself had instituted. This indicated a decisive break with the old way of life: dying to the old in the waters of baptism, they rose up, symbolically, to the new life in Christ. It was an unmistakeable, unrepeatable, and unquestionably a highly significant step, often neglected nowadays in some circles. But the first Christians saw repentance, faith, reception of the Spirit and baptism, as very much a *unity*. New Christians need to be baptised. Those who join up with Christ have a right to wear the uniform.

The early Christians gave great care to teaching the new converts (Acts 2:42). First it must have been teaching about Jesus, the sort of material we have in the Gospels. Then it concerned the new life in Christ and the different and distinctive lifestyle that the Holy Spirit gradually produces in Christian people, the sort of thing we find in the Epistles. The primary teachers were the apostles themselves, and their message is now enshrined for our use in the New Testament. So the new believer needs to be taught how to handle and feed on the Word.

There was a good deal of emphasis on fellowship (literally a *"joint participation in"*) Jesus and his program (Acts 2:42). This clearly took three forms. *First,* personal attention by a more experienced Christian friend, the sort of thing Barnabas did with Paul or Paul did with Silvanus. This personal meeting-up is vital in a new Christian's early days, and provides an opportunity for doubts to be aired and difficulties handled. *Second,* there was the fellowship of the small group. We see it in Acts 13:1 for instance, but it was a regular feature in early Christianity. We rarely find anyone functioning on his own: one is normally in the company of a small group. And *third,* of course, the fellowship of the wider community, the church, which is the Body of Christ, in which your friend is a new body part.

These early people who in massive historical fact turned their world (*cruel* world) upside down stressed the importance of worship (Acts 2:42), particularly the "breaking of bread" or Holy Communion. It is not difficult for the newest Christian to understand that the broken bread represents Christ's body broken for them, the wine Christ's poured-out blood, and their heart will be warmed in gratitude. There is of course great depth in this sacrament, but if he or she understands just this much it is not a bad start.

And they made prayer a priority (Acts 2:42). The one mark given to Ananias of the dreaded Saul of Tarsus having become a new man was this: "he is praying" (Acts 9:11). There are many questions about prayer to be carefully answered as they crop up, but it is vital to help the new believer start praying at once, privately and together with you – which will lead to his or her praying without embarrassment in a group. Indeed, the most natural translation of Acts 2:42 is "at the prayer times."

The apostles insisted on public witness to Christ: "we are all witnesses" (Acts 2:32). Public witness to Jesus was normal in the early church, as it is in much of Africa and the East today, but it needs to be rediscovered in the West. New believers grow when they take a bold stand for Christ, and they need to be helped to discern when that is appropriate.

Finally, I am very struck by the way pastoral oversight was a priority to the first Christians. They really looked after young Christians. I think we can assume that it was normal for every Mark to have his Peter, every Timothy his Paul. Pastoral care is one of the gifts of God to his church (Eph 4:11). Leaders are meant to equip the saints for service (Eph 4:12) and in the New Testament we find them doing just that by setting an example, exercising discipline, taking young Christians as assistants on missions, writing them letters. Initial doubts need to be addressed, a devotional life established, ethical issues discussed, and dealing with a host of problems which inevitably arise, and where a guide and mentor is invaluable.

CONTENTS

CONTENTS

CONTENTS

The Way Forward

Nurturing New Believers

The *Christian Foundations* Course

Michael Green

Anglican House
Publishers

them? Is there some opportunity or area of Christian service for which his or her gifts particularly equip them?

And of course you will want to make it plain that they are always welcome to telephone or come for a chat with you, even long after the course is over.

The Talk

Probably the main leader should give the talk for the first two weeks in the interest of competence and continuity. As the overall leader, your talk must set up the *single theme* of the evening, and portray that theme succinctly, coherently, and attractively. The theme of the evening will be identical for its three elements: the talk, the scripture verse to be learned, and the inductive Bible study, so that each element – *the talk, the scripture verse, and the Bible study* – reinforces the others.

I do not offer sample talks. *Preparing the talk is your job*! You will want to make the material your own because that is what will give your talk life and impact! I will be making some suggestions for the talks' content, but there is much more that you could use topically. Importantly, you will want to be very selective in what you put in and omit, choosing *only* what the members of the group need to come to grips with if they are to flourish in their new Christian life. *Less is more* in this case!

Your talk must be simple and appealing, avoiding clichés and churchy language. It has got to be clearly understood by people, many of whom may have no background whatsoever. You will need to grab their attention and hold it for 10 minutes while you speak. Anything longer is unwise! Try to speak not just so that people can understand but so that nobody can possibly *misunderstand* you. Use scripture but not too much, and don't attempt cross references or you will be bound to lose some people as they scrabble around in Numbers when seeking a reference in Acts!

And try to leave some loose ends to provoke questions when you are done. There may not be many the first week, but they will grow. You need to be discerning. Let some of their comments in a question time pass you by without any additions by you. But fasten on to one or two here and there, enlarge upon them a bit, and make them into teaching points.

The Verse Learning

Your aim in this is to enable them to know six verses of scripture, by heart, with their reference, by the end of the course. Why? *"Your word have I hid in my heart that I might not sin against you"* said the psalmist in 119:1. Learning verses of scripture has sadly fallen out of fashion these days, assisted by the plethora of modern translations, but to lodge bits of scripture in the heart is a vital way to grow both in grace and understanding.

I sometimes introduce it like this, "Okay folks, what we are going to do now may be very unfamiliar to you. We are going to actually learn an important verse from the Bible each week. You will find it coming back into

TWO

The Leaders

A good deal depends on the leaders of a course like this. They need to be relational and warm, folk who enjoy being with people. And shared leadership of the group is wise, almost essential, if there is to be good pastoral care of each individual. The overall leader of the little leadership team needs to be somewhat experienced in Christian teaching and fairly well informed on the questions people have and the difficulties they experience as they start out on the Christian life. But his or her colleagues do not need to have much experience, or even much Bible knowledge. They just need to know Christ and be excited about Him! Indeed, it is sometimes an advantage to have as one of the leaders a person who is a pretty new Christian and might even have gone through the course themselves recently.

All the leaders must know how to lead someone to Christ, and they need to be familiar with the course material. They need to know how to run a small group studying the Bible in such a way that all of the participants contribute. I am persuaded of the value of a little "leadership team" rather than a single leader. This "team" could simply consist of two leaders with somewhat complementary strengths; for example, one leader perhaps being stronger on the teaching side and the other better at putting people at their ease. Sometimes with a larger group of about a dozen members, I have worked with three fellow leaders. The proportion of leaders to members is a determining factor in the success of the course. Your leaders will all be laypeople likely with regular jobs and perhaps families, and they simply will not have the time to give proper attention and pastoral care to more than two or at most three members of the group.

Personal care and the occasional helpful private chat is vital for the development of new Christians. They need to be made to feel that they matter, that someone is concerned about them, and that there is a safe place to unload doubts and difficulties that they would not air in the group meetings. That is why shared leadership is important.

Shared leadership also enables the overall leader to sense how his colleagues are getting on. He may find out that this service is not the right niche for someone who might fit better into another area of Christian ministry in future. On the other hand, one may show all the gifts that qualify them to run the group next time round.

In a church where I once ministered we ran many of these groups, and in due course we built up a core of 60 leaders from among whom to draw when

This Short Course

There are recorded ways in which apostolic age Christians sought to nurture new believers, and by any comparison to them our own casual efforts are absolutely lamentable. This little book is written to help remedy that contemporary weakness. It is a short *Foundation Course* for new Christians, and is written for the benefit of any who will give themselves up to leading such a course.

This short course has been extensively tested in both church and university settings, in England and in America. It is specifically designed to help the newest believer to get a grasp on the basics of their faith, and then to grow in Christ – and by the grace of God it has proved to be very fruitful. It is aimed primarily at those who have recently come to personal faith in Christ (and also for those seeking such a faith).

This course is not intended for the sceptical agnostic on the one hand or for the established Christian on the other. Both of these people tend to disturb the dynamics of a group made up of people struggling to find Christ and to grow in him. Thus the course stands as a *bridge* between the non-Christian or the merely nominal church member, on the one hand, and those who enjoy the warm relationships of Christian fellowship on the other. Normally at the end of this course, participants will rather seamlessly transfer into one of the Christian fellowship groups regularly to be found in most good churches and on college and university campuses.

This *Christian Foundations Course* in as many weeks covers six areas that are the essential building blocks for a well functioning Christian life – *Commitment to Christ, Assurance, Growth, Christian Fellowship, the Holy Spirit,* and *Witness And Service.*

This list of Christian essentials could easily be extended, but it is deliberately kept short – *people tend to drop off of long courses.* Each evening session consists of four elements: a short talk by the leader (with questions); a single verse of scripture to memorise; a passage of scripture on the topic for the evening (to study as a group); and the opportunity for short prayers or thanksgivings. (Most people will soon be comfortable about praying aloud and giving thanks.) This simple format encourages participants to seek answers during the few weeks.

It is important to make time for nibbles and drinks in the circulating time – as folks come in, questions are asked, news of some new discovery or answer to prayer they've experienced is shared, and especially in the first couple of weeks – as an ice-breaker to relax people and enable them to mix. They usually bond quickly and won't be in any hurry to leave at the end of a session, and that itself provides excellent initial discovery of Christian fellowship – perhaps before they have even heard those two words! It also gives the leaders a natural opportunity for spending time with their charges, and for making mental notes of any needs to be addressed later at a suitable time.

the rescue" (Matthew 1:21). He is the fulfilment of God's self-revelation (John 1:18; Hebrews 1:1). He is helpfully described as God's "Word" to us, God's message in terms of a human life (John 1:1-4,14). This Jesus is the cosmic Christ, head of the universe as he is of the church (Colossians 1:15-18). He is the same yesterday, today, and forever (Hebrews 13:8).

What did he do? Why did he come?

Jesus lived a perfect life. He healed and taught. His impact was phenomenal, arousing hostility from the clergy of that day which eventually led to his death on the cross. He knew this was coming and said he would give his life as a ransom for many (Mark 10:45).

Peter explained the meaning of the cross with great clarity (1Peter 3:18). Jesus absorbed the filth of human sin so as to make a way back to God possible for any of us. And we need it, because all humans have this disease of sin; that is, of self-centredness (Romans 3:23). It is a disease that has fatal consequences, because sin spoils lives (Jeremiah 17:9), imposes a bondage (John 8:34), separates from a holy God (Isaiah 59:1,2), and is *fatal* if not dealt with (Romans 6:23).

Not only did Jesus come to lay down his life for us, but to break the power of sin and death by his resurrection that first Easter day. He returned to heaven, his work completed, and now comes with the power of the Holy Spirit to indwell believers (Philippians 4:13).

You will need to be very selective in what you choose to say about all this. Some of it will be covered in later meetings. On this first night you'll want to give only a brisk overview, because you need to give proper time and maximum clarity to the fourth question.

How do I get in touch?

Relationship with God is restored by taking four steps:

Admit that I am not currently in touch with God; that I am self-centred; that I need to change, would welcome a fresh ability to overcome my weak points, and am deeply sorry for having alienated God by my behaviour and attitude.

Believe that God in the person of Christ came to this earth to find the likes of me, went to the cross to deal with man's guilt, mine included, and is risen from the dead, alive, and available.

Consider the cost of becoming a Christian. I will need to welcome Jesus not just as Saviour or rescuer but as Lord; that is, as boss in every part of my life. Realize I must expect some opposition if I become his follower. What's more, I'll need to be open about my commitment to his cause, and I will need to link up with his followers. It's costly, really, to become a Christian. But it is more costly not to.

Do it! It takes two to establish a partnership. God has done all that is necessary on his side. So I need to respond, and invite the Spirit of the risen Christ into my life. He will come as Saviour to cleanse and forgive me, as Lord to control and empower me, and as Friend to be with me always.

I find Revelation 3:20 the clearest description of how to invite someone into the life, and I'll make very sure that I have left time to explain it.

In this relaxed atmosphere I don't attempt to make an appeal of any sort. I simply mention the booklets on commitment they can pick up as they leave.

Whilst repentance and faith is the personal side of it (and baptism is the public mark of Christian initiation) it is only when a person receives the Holy Spirit that they fully become a Christian. (More in Section EIGHT)

The Verse To Learn

For this first evening I choose Revelation 3:20. It encapsulates the theme of the evening, *The Heart Of The Matter.* On the principle that a picture is worth a thousand words, it can be helpful to show them Holman Hunt's painting *The Light of the World,* where the symbolism of the house, the weeds, the Visitor, the lantern, and the absence of handle on the outside of the door (*it can be opened only from the inside*), is poignant and self-explanatory. You might have on hand a few postcards of it that you can buy on the internet for less than $1, so they can hold it in their hands and really absorb it.

The Bible Study

We have seen in the previous chapter how to go about leading a small group Bible study without dominating it. The whole idea is to encourage the participants to find treasures in the Bible passage for themselves. Naturally the passage for this first night will be to show that the commitment to Christ we've been talking about is deeply rooted in the New Testament itself. For this we could have selected the conversion of St. Paul in Acts 9, or Jesus' dialogue about the new birth with Nicodemus in John 3, but I prefer to use the Zacchaeus story in Luke 19:1-10. It is straightforward and very vivid. Introduce it in a way such as this, once they have found the place. "We are going to look at an unpopular man in a compromising job. His name was Zacchaeus, and his life was a mess, but he very much wanted to meet with Jesus, who was due to pass through his home town, Jericho, for the last time before going to his death in Jerusalem. Let's see what happened when Zacchaeus welcomed Jesus to his home, and the great results that flowed from it. There will be a lot we can identify with."

That is more than enough to get them going. Pray for them for insight. Have a silent couple of minutes to get them searching, and then see what they come up with. Welcome any and all contributions – because it will be costly for them to say anything this first evening.

Here are some of the questions you may find helpful if contributions dry up. (No need to use them if not!)

FOUR

The Heart Of The Matter

You have a lot of ground to cover – at a pace the members can cope with – and the thing is you will be dealing with concepts that are unfamiliar, even jarring, to some or all of the group!

The Talk

Your *10 minute* (Not longer!) talk will need to be warm and attractive, but also *very* carefully planned. Obviously this requires real time and thought on your part. Unless you are rather well experienced in this sort of thing, you may want to go ahead and practice it for another of the leaders beforehand.

You may want to explain briefly that the Bible is the Handbook of Christianity, and that you will be using it each week. Then, on to the opening talk, bearing in mind that it will be reinforcement to for those who have already committed themselves to Christ, but *news* to some of the others!

You may care to base your talk round four questions, and there will only be time to touch on them briefly. I am suggesting suitable scripture verses for you to choose from, if you wish, but you will need to use your own discretion as to where the emphasis should lie and how much you should include. And remember, a surfeit of good things on the first night might exhaust some of your newbies, to the extent you might not see them again!

The questions you may want to cover are these:

What is Christianity?

Real Christianity is not so much a religion, as a revelation, a rescue, and a relationship. Historically, religions have been man's way of trying to get through to God. *Revelation* is God's way to get through to man! He has revealed himself throughout the Bible, primarily as *Creator* (Genesis 1:1), *Holy* (Isaiah 6:3) and *Love* (1John 4:8). But human beings are rebels against God's love, and determined to go their own way. This breaks God's heart, so in his great love he resolved to find a rescue for us. He did this by coming to find us in Christ (John 3:16).

Christianity therefore must not be confused with churchgoing, ceremonies, creeds or conduct, though it embraces all four. Christianity is *Christ*!

Who is Jesus Christ?

He was (and ever lives as) fully human, but more than human. His very name – *Jesus* – means "God to

The Verse To Learn

After the talk there will usually be questions, but probably these will not flow much on the first night. So I go on to teach them the verse of scripture, one that is memorable and fits the theme for the evening. It may help to ease the strangeness of this by kidding them that they are back in Sunday School (or doing their penance for not having had to attend Sunday School!), and then they won't object. But I find they really do not mind anyway. People seem to realise intuitively that it's going to help them to have a few verses of the Bible tucked away in their memory.

The Bible Study

Unless the group numbers half a dozen or less you would be wise to split them up into two groups for the inductive Bible study passage, which has, of course, been pre-selected to fit in with the theme of the evening. You may let people split randomly, or not, though it is a good idea to see to it that husbands and wives go into different groups. Alternatively, you may prefer to organise who goes into which group. I slightly prefer this way of doing it because, having listened to why members have come, you can keep the more difficult ones in your group, and let your less experienced assistant leaders take on the more promising lot. It also allows that if some have already made it clear that they have committed themselves to Christ, you can distribute them between the two groups, which will prove very helpful as the weeks go by. At all events, be clear beforehand with your fellow leaders which of these procedures you will be adopting.

The two groups will go into separate rooms, or if the room is quite large, to separate areas that are out of earshot. They'll pick up the Bibles provided, and have about 25 minutes to do the study. The first evening it is likely to be less than 25 minutes for this because you will have used time having everyone introduce themselves. There is likely to be some panic for some as they sit there with this unfamiliar book in their hands, and it is your job as a leader to dispel it speedily. This is where you will realise what a good idea it is to have copies of the same version of the Bible for them all.

Ignorance of the Bible is so widespread nowadays that you may like to say something like "The Bible in your hands is a big book, made up of two 'halves' or testaments. We are going to look at a passage in the second half tonight, called the New Testament, the first part being the Old Testament." Then announce the page number, and tell them how many verses you are going to read. When they have all found the place, you might want to give a couple of sentences explaining the context and purpose of the passage, before asking a fellow leader to offer a short prayer for God to make the passage come alive. The psalmist was right when he prayed "Lord, open my eyes that I may behold wonderful things from your law." We should follow his example.

Get each of the group to read a verse or two of the passage, in order to enable scripture make its own impact on them. Give them a full minute to read over the whole passage again to themselves, and to choose a verse or bit of a verse that really strikes them. I say "Let's each choose the bit of this that we find to be quite striking – it might be a promise, or perhaps a challenge, or even something entirely new to our understanding, or whatever – and then we'll share it with one another for a minute or so, saying what we have chosen and why we like it." At the end of the minute or two of silence you've suggested (if they manage to keep quiet that long!) ask who is going to start, and what verse they are bringing us. Generally it takes off, but some people will remain silent for a week or two. This is not a problem. Let them settle in to it and then maybe ask them a question in week three. But of course there will be times when "contributions" dry up, and you will need to produce some good questions to stimulate discussion and show how to apply the Bible to real life. Having some questions "at the ready" is a big part of a leader's preparation, and I have provided a few for each evening.

The Prayer Time

We have seen in the previous chapter how easy it becomes to have the group transition from "pooling" their insights about the Bible passage to turning these into prayers. But it is new and rather scary to them. So I often initiate this idea on the first evening by saying "Look, we have been talking *about* the Lord all evening. Let's end by talking *to* him, shall we? It's not difficult to do so, even out loud. You can speak to each other can't you? – So speak to him. You might like to thank him for something you have liked in this passage, or ask him to make something needful come true in your life." This will be strange to them, and so keep it short on the first evening, if you risk it at all.

Prayer will be developing as weeks go by. Close the prayer time yourself, and the business of the evening is then over. You have finished on time as you had promised and people are free to go. But often they will want to hang around. The other half of the group returns, and you enjoy some chat before they all drift away. So a refill of the drinks and a bit more to eat or maybe some ice cream will help towards the atmosphere of welcome and hospitality that you want to create and sustain.

The Review

Now you and your colleagues can sit down, breathe a sigh of relief, and hear how the other Bible reading went, if you have split into two groups. You'll go through the evening to see what could be improved, and to reflect on what each person has said in their introduction. This will give you a good idea of which leader should look after which member of the group pastorally. At all events, divide them up among yourselves after that first night, so you leaders can pray intensively for them, and see more of them in your own time. Finally, planning for next week needs to be firmed up. The evening ends with the leaders thanking God and offering any short prayers for this or that person, before the leaders, too, go home.

1. Why do you think Zacchaeus felt the need to meet Jesus? Why do we?

2. Why did Jesus bother about Zacchaeus? How long do you think it was since anyone had gone to dinner with Zacchaeus?

3. Did Zacchaeus have to smarten his life up before Jesus would enter his house?

4. What does Jesus bring when he comes into someone's life?

5. What difference did Jesus' visit make to Zacchaeus?

The Prayer Time

You will probably be surprised and thrilled by some of the contributions, and may well be moved by the simple one-sentence prayers that one or two of them may utter on this first evening in the group, should you feel it right to suggest that they may utter a simple prayer if any are led to so do.

The Review

See the end of the previous chapter.

so they know where they are. It is important to stick to it too! Then I observe how remarkable it is that here we are – a group of people who do not know one another, but have met to talk about God, on a weekday evening, in a private home or other venue. (That's no less than *four* surprises!) So I suggest it would be good to go around the group to briefly introduce ourselves and explain what has brought us here.

I'll say, "Perhaps, having suggested it, I had better start off." And then I give a brief version of the story of my encounter with Christ, which has proved the best thing that ever happened to me *and* something I am keen to share with others. I then turn to one of my fellow leaders, seated on my left, and he tells just a bit of his story and why he is here. Now the members have had a couple of models of the sort of thing that is wanted, and are perfectly happy to go round the group and say why they have come. Make it plain that all comments are welcome and acceptable, whatever background they are coming from, and whether or not they are believers. This enables people to feel safe and speak freely. Assure them that this kind of sharing is a one-off, and will not be repeated in the following weeks.

Of course, you and your fellow leaders will listen to all this with your ears cocked. What they say will give you an initial idea of where they're coming from spiritually; whether they are committed to Christ yet, or are seeking him; whether they are confused about the whole thing, or really just don't know what drew them here. This information, stored in your memory, may be significant in deciding how you split them up for the Bible reading part of the evening, and will certainly be a useful starting point when you come to have the one-to-one chats later.

Time For Your Talk

Now it's time to give the short talk that you have prepared, and there is a lot to be said for the main leader doing it the first couple of weeks. Interesting as your talk is, it is important not to let this go on too long, because you have a great deal to accomplish in a short evening. You must be yourself and do it in your own way, but it is important to be relaxed and relational, showing clearly what Christianity is not and what it really is. (I've suggested some of the components of this very first talk in the next chapter, but it must be *your* talk.)

In my talks I'll explain very briefly our human predicament of alienation from God, what God has done to rectify it, and of course I'll close with his offer of reconciliation. So I seek to outline the gospel succinctly and clearly, but not to press for a decision at this time. Remember, some of them will already have made that commitment, and you'll have five more weeks ahead of you in which others can weigh up their response and make it in their own time. I do mention however that we've placed some copies of a booklet explaining the way to Christ by the door, so people can pick one up as they leave. (I confess that I count them before putting them out and love to see how many disappear!)

THREE

The First Evening

This first meeting is absolutely crucial. Lose them tonight and you've probably lost them for good. *Intrigue* them now and they will come every week. It is impossible to exaggerate how important it is that the evening goes well.

Preparations

In addition to praying for each "customer" with your team beforehand, it is well worth phoning each person assigned to your group, and also sending an email reminding them of the time and place. This is particularly important with young singles or students, who tend to live a day at a time and are not exactly brilliant at remembering an engagement they agreed to three or four days ahead of time!

Meet up with your colleagues half-an-hour before you expect any of the group to come. Ensure you all know who is doing what for the evening, and make any last minute preparations. You will have your talk ready, you will have chosen the verse for learning, and deployed your team on "door" and "coffee" squads. You will have your Bibles (identical ones!) ready so that each member can borrow one. And you may or may not have decided on a small "bookstall" as suggested in the previous chapter.

If there are more than two or three people coming you should provide nametags for them for the first couple of meetings at least.

And you wait for them to come. Wait *Joyfully!*

Starting Out

As the principal leader do make sure that you chat warmly with each one in the "hospitality period" when folks are coming in. This should last about ten minutes to allow for varying arrival times, but not longer or people will decide it isn't worth coming until a quarter of an hour or more after the advertised time. And if that happens it will disrupt things not a little.

When they are all there and had some refreshment you may want to use an icebreaker of some sort. "Everyone, shake hands with the nearest person and tell them you're glad they're here!" Or whatever. Then set out the chairs in a circle, and you are ready to start the meeting.

Introductions

I like to begin by welcoming them and assuring them what time the meeting will be over every week,

You may decide to bring a little box of books suitable to each evening's theme – together with one or two Bibles, and *Newness of Life* notes – to give, lend or sell. If so the best time to mention this is before the Bible reading. Otherwise you just move straight from *The Verse Learning* into *The Inductive Bible Study*.

professions of faith called for the launch of another new group! (It's always wise to have your baskets in position before you shake the tree for apples to fall!)

Leaders' Responsibilities

Let's have an overview of just what leading the *Short Course*, or one's helping in the leadership, will involve. Before the course starts, the leaders need to get together to discover each other's spiritual story and strengths. For instance, one may have been reared in a Christian home and have grown into Christ that way. Another may have had more of a crisis conversion. Both will find members of the group who will have had a similar story, and that could provide a pointer to which leader should pair up with which group member for pastoral care. Or one leader may have had a scientific background while another's background was in literature, which would make it obvious who should respond to the different types of questions that are sure to emerge during the meetings. If the leaders are of a different gender or race or color, that is an advantage. The point is they will be called on to complement each other, and function in concert. This itself is excellent modelling for the members of the group to observe, and in due course to emulate.

So before the group starts, the leaders get together, share their stories and begin to sense how they can make the most of their partnership. They will obviously need to pray over every name that has been submitted to them, and they will meet several times to do this before the group arrives. They will also want to give careful thought to the planning of the first meeting –

who will host the event, have the coffee ready, who will be on the door to welcome, who will give the talk, who will teach the verse, and who will lead the inductive Bible study.

Having the principal leader host the meetings in their home should be avoided. It's more than a little distracting to try to function as an attentive host while having to keep your focus where it ought to be at all times. You wouldn't distract a surgeon at work!

The Venue

The room has to be got ready. I think it is best not to have armchairs, or indeed too many chairs at all set out initially. Because you want people to get coffee or tea, water or a soft drink and begin to mix with one another. If two flop onto a couch you can't get to talk to them, nor do they get to talk with anyone else. I like to have a pile of stacked chairs ready, and ten minutes after the advertised start, when people have circulated and chatted a bit, only then is the time to put the chairs out in a circle, and get people to sit down.

It is a good idea to have a stack of Bibles ready, all in the same translation (perhaps borrowed from a local church if the meeting is out of town). This enables you to turn people to a particular page rather than give them a Bible reference, making it easy for "newbies" to quickly find their place. It also avoids the annoyance of people with various versions wasting time by chirping up, "My version says..." The NIV and ESV are the modern translations most widely used these days, so it might be wise to agree one of them.

FIVE

Assurance

You can't build a satisfactory house on an insecure foundation, and you can't build a fulfilled Christian life if you are not sure you *belong*. However, a great many Christians are very unsure of their standing. They may be looking at the quality of their good deeds and wondering if they're good enough. They may feel it is arrogant to say "I know I am a Christian."

As soon as a person entrusts their life to Christ they are invariably assailed with doubts. That is the Tempter's prime method of unsettling new Christians. We have got to provide them with help. So this second week's meeting is very important.

There are many images in scripture of Christ and the believer getting together. It may be "to receive him," "to come to him," "to put on Christ," or "to drink his living water" and many more. It does not matter which image we go for. They all speak of us, in our need, and Christ, in his sufficiency, coming together. But is the relationship permanent? Can I be sure of him? That is the question that nags at the heart of the new believer.

The skilled pastor will want to discover what it is that is troubling the convert, and show how scripture provides solid assurance.

One may be wondering if his or her life is good enough for God. As one person who professed faith just last night in my presence put it, "Will he like me? I have done some pretty terrible things." But the promise of the Saviour is "Whoever comes to me I will never, no never cast out" (John 6:37). [The force of the Greek double negative is very, very powerful. "It will never, ever, no way happen!"] Or I think of the man who was a sniper in war and had killed many people in cold blood. Would God hold his past evil actions against him, he wondered? He found peace when he saw the truth of Romans 8:1 (No condemnation for those who are in Christ Jesus).

Often young believers get the impression that if they sin as a Christian (as one assuredly will) they will get thrown out of God's family, and will need to ask Christ back in all over again. We can show them 1John 1:9, "If we (the letter is written to Christians) confess our sins God is faithful (because he promised) and just (because the debt has been settled at Calvary) to forgive us our sins and to cleanse us from all unrighteousness." That's why when we sin we should run to Jesus, not from him. Christ, once welcomed in the heart and life, will never leave us nor forsake us (Hebrews 13:5).

"Can I keep it up, this Christian life?" is another way that doubt afflicts new Christians. No, of course none of us can "keep it up" on our own, but the Lord is able to keep us up, and that's a different matter (1Peter 1:5).

New believers become acutely aware of temptation in ways they never were before. "How can I overcome temptation?" is the cry. 1Corinthians 10:13 is the reply. Three things: Our temptations are common to others; God will not allow us to be overwhelmed; And with every temptation comes his way of escape, so we can be able to cope with them.

With such hesitations in mind, how could we best address this topic of assurance? Can new believers be made really sure that God accepts them?

The Talk

God is so keen that we should know where we stand that the whole Trinity combines to assure us.

The Word of God the Father is something we can trust. He gives his testimony that "whoever has the Son has life." 1 John 5:10-12

The Work of God the Son is unrepeatable and lasting. "God loved us and sent the Son to be the atoning sacrifice for our sins." 1John 4:10 The job is finished.

And, *The witness of God the Holy Spirit* is unmistakeable. "This is how we know he lives in us, by the Spirit that he has given us." 1John 3:24 The Spirit gradually makes himself known to a new believer in a number of ways, and the letter of 1John tells us what they are. The Spirit breeds in us:

New desire to please God – 2:24

New assurance of our being forgiven – 1:9; 2:1,2

New willingness to face opposition – 3:13

New delight being with other Christians – 3:14

New generosity of spirit – 3:17

New experience of overcoming temptation – 4:4;5:4

New discovery that God answers prayer – 3:22

New priorities – 5:21

These marks of the Spirit's presence do not all come at once, or in any particular order. They are like bulbs that the Spirit plants in the soil of our lives, and they produce a variety of flowers, coming up at different times. We are not meant to guess or hope that we belong. We are meant to *know* that! "I write this to you who believe in the name of the Son of God, so that you may know that you have eternal life" (5:13).

After the talk, questions are likely to flow more readily than last week because people are getting used to each other. Tonight can be a most valuable time.

The Verse To Learn

1John 5:12. "Whoever has the Son has life: whoever does not have the Son of God does not have life."

Nothing could be clearer. If you have welcomed the Son of God into your life, you already have the first instalment of eternal life. Death will only enlarge it.

The Bible Study

It might be good to use the story of Saul's conversion on this second evening in the group. Some aspects of it were unique, but much of it applies to everyone who discovers Jesus. It is found in Acts 9:1-22. You could introduce it by saying that the man we are going to look at tonight was the fiercest and maybe cruelest opponent of early Christianity, but when he welcomed the Lord into his life he turned into its most passionate advocate – and it is fascinating to see how he gradually became sure that he belonged.

Some helpful questions for you to use, but only if contributions dry up:

1. Saul was certainly intelligent and well educated, religious, virtuous, enthusiastic and sincere. Surely a person like that needs no conversion, then or now?
2. Later on Saul called his conversion a "pattern" or an "example" (1Timothy 1:16). In what ways was this true?
3. Was there any "Ananias'" to help you start your journey to Jesus?
4. What differences in his life convinced Saul and others that the change in him was real?
5. What struck you most in this story?

The Prayer Time

Prayer will come more easily this second evening. Encourage them each to choose from the passage "One thing you've learned," and "One verse that particularly struck you."

Then you might ask, "Can you make a prayer about each of these?" We have been reading about being in God's family, and being confident about it. God has no dumb children, and he wants us to talk to him just as naturally as we talk with one another. *In family life all the members join in the conversation!* Praying aloud is of course no more valuable than praying silently, but it helps us concentrate on what we are saying, and it enables others to join in the *Amen*. "So let's each of us try a one sentence prayer of thanks, or a request, or a thought from the Bible passage."

The Review

It is important that the first pastoral chat happens soon. By the end of this second evening you and your fellow leaders will have a much better ideas of how people are progressing, and whether your fellow leaders are happy with the members provisionally allotted to them for pastoral care, or if they sense that they likely cannot get close to them.

You could entrust a fellow leader with giving the talk or teaching the verse of scripture next week, giving him or her help as needed.

Naturally the leaders will pray for each of the members and for each other before leaving for the evening.

SIX

Growing As A Christian

This evening will concentrate on our devotional life. But it is important to grow in friendship within the group. So you might begin the evening by getting them to talk together about something that has excited or discouraged them this week.

We all know about some of the requirements for having healthy bodies, such as good food, fresh air, cleanliness, exercise, and so forth. The Christian life has counterparts for all these. Your talk might reflect this. Or you may decide to handle it entirely differently!

So don't be afraid to depart from the following suggestion for your talk, if you are so led and are putting the right amount of time and attention into it.

The Talk

Good Food / *The Bible*

The Bible is a collection of 66 books by 40 authors superintended by the Holy Spirit and originally written in three languages and in a variety of literary styles (prose, history, poetry, biography, straight instruction, etc.). It is more of a little library than a book. It is good food. Second Timothy 3:14-17 is very clear on the origin and purpose of the Bible. You may want to have them find it and read it to them. The Bible's main theme is salvation – God's intervention in our world to rescue us from our self-centredness. It shows us what God is like and how much he wants us to relate to him. It describes itself as a *mirror* (James 1:22-25), a *sword* (Ephesians 6:17), a *hammer* (Jeremiah 23:29), *sweetness* (Ezekiel 3:3) and *milk* (1 Peter 2:2).

It is vital for us to read it – and to keep on reading it regularly – if we want to grow as Christians, since it can *nourish* us (1Peter 2:2), *cleanse* us (Psalm119:9), *guide* us (Psalm119:105) and give us *peace* and *wisdom* (Psalm 119:165; Proverbs 4:4-6) and *keep us in touch with Jesus* (John15:7).

How should they go about reading it? The first thing is to acquire a good modern version (NIV, ESV, Good News Bible, etc.) and get a scheme that provides some helpful notes, like the *Scripture Union, Every Day with Jesus* or the *Bible Reading Fellowship.*

Then, asking for God's illumination, they can get started by reading a passage slowly a couple of times, looking for a *promise* to claim, a *command* to obey, *warnings* to heed, a *prayer* we could use, and *examples* of good or bad behaviour. They could usefully ask themselves three questions:

What did this mean originally?

How does it apply to me?

Should I turn what I have found into prayer?

It would be gracious to give each member a copy of *Newness of Life* (available from *10ofthose.com*) to get them started on personal Bible reading and prayer.

Fresh Air / *Prayer*

Prayer has many sides to it. We can think of it as tuning into God or having a conversation with him. In prayer we discover something of his mind (Ephesians 5:10,17) and join in his purposes (Matthew 9:35 and 10:1,6). Prayer includes:

Worship – Rejoicing in his wonder and love
(Psalm 96:7,8)

Confession – Getting rid of the blotches
(Psalm 32:3-5)

Thanksgiving – For his forgiveness and generosity
(Psalm 103:1-5)

Meditation – Reflecting on scripture
(Psalm 119:48)

Interceding – Prayer for other people, situations
(Romans 1:9f)

Offering Ourselves – Unto him for his service
(Romans 12:1,2)

Listening – Ask his Spirit for a prompt how to pray (Romans 8:26)

There are various ways to learn how to pray. We can learn by doing it regularly (Daniel 6:10) or by "arrow prayers" (Matthew 14:30). We can do it alone (Mark 1:35) or with others (Matthew 18:20). Another way we can learn is directly from Jesus – the prayer he taught (Luke 11:1-13) and the way he prayed (John 17). Of course, we can also learn from books and from other Christians. The great thing is to make a regular time for prayer when you won't be distracted, and then stick to it of course.

It is easy to get discouraged when prayer seems to go unanswered. If that is the case it is good to ask oneself some questions. Do I really pray? (James 4:2) And mean it? (Matthew 7:7). Are my goals selfish? (James 4:3) Do I persevere in prayer? (Luke 18:1-8) Am I seeking God's will? (Mark 14:36) Answers may not always come in the form or at the time we expect. The answer may be "No" or '"Wait."

Cleanliness / *Confession*

Unconfessed sin spoils our relationship with God. Period! (Isaiah 59:1,2) Our calling is to be clean in our thinking, in our speech, and in our behaviour (1Peter 1:13-16), and to come back and ask God for cleansing when we fail (Psalm 32:1-5).

Exercise / *Christian Service*

No Christian is too new to ask God "How would you like me to work for you by helping other people?"

The Verse To Learn

Psalm 119:105 "Your word is a lamp to my feet and a light for my path." What a wonderful assurance of the relevance of scripture to our daily lives!

The Bible Study

Colossians 1:3-14 This is a magnificent passage that both makes scripture live and shows how Paul prayed for other Christians – indeed for Christians that he had never even met! Let them dig in this rich mine, but here are some questions if things dry up:

1. Why is thanksgiving such an important part of prayer?
2. What are the main things Paul asks for? How should we pray for our friends?
3. Paul prays that they may know God's power. What sort of things is that power meant to achieve?
4. What are the main marks of discipleship here?

The Prayer Time

Encourage them all to think for a moment about the things they have discussed and then join in prayer out loud, including prayer by name for some of their friends.

Before they go, suggest a bring-and-share supper for next week. They will each wonder what to bring. Tell them that the good Lord will make a splendid meal of whatever they bring. They will find it hard to believe – but next week they will discover it is true.

your mind from time to time and helping you in your Christian life. Tonight we are going to learn (give the verse you've selected). I'm going to read it, say a word of explanation, and then we are going to read it together, out loud, with its reference (that is, its "address" so that you can find it again). Then we will read it aloud a second time. And then again once more, but this time you will do it without me!" Then I'll say this, "Right, you should have it by now. But watch out (*with a chuckle)* "I am going to test you on it next week." I have never, ever had a complaint about this!

The Inductive Bible Study

The aim of *inductive* instruction is not for the teacher to teach the students anything, but to enable the students to learn for themselves. You conduct an *Inductive Bible Study* by introducing and explaining scriptures, and expecting the members of the group to complete some tasks to absorb them. Each time you will have planned to use a relatively short passage of scripture containing no more that about a half-dozen verses, enough to instruct but not too much for them to absorb and understand.

If you have a group of more than about six, split it in two, and get a co-leader or leaders to take some of them off into the kitchen or wherever, while you and another leader handle the remainder of the group. Make sure everyone has one of the Bibles you've stashed away. Announce the page number. Wait until they have all found it. And then invite a fellow leader to offer a short prayer asking for understanding.

You want the page to spring to life and impact the hearts and minds of your "customers." You also want to provide a model for them to follow in their own Bible study once they get that going. Have them read the passage aloud, so that they get used to the sound of their own voices reading scripture in a private house or whatever venue, on a weekday, (which can be quite a shock!). Suggest a minute or two of silence so that each person can fasten on the verse they like or are most gripped by. Wait your full minute and then open it up for discussion.

You are going to need to remain very disciplined, because it is so easy for you to explain it to them, but you want them to find it for themselves. Hens grow better and stronger if they have to scratch around for food and not get fed all the time by the farmer! More on this in a later chapter, but watch the clock, and close the contributions two or three minutes before the closing time that you announced.

Suggest that your charges might like to pray short, one-sentences prayers of thanks or request, based on the passage they've studied. Just a sentence is plenty long enough. And encourage all of them to back up the person praying with a heartfelt *Amen*, which is a sort of Hebrew signature tune meaning, "Yes! I back that!" Encourage participation but do not press it. Stop rather before you want to. After a little tell them you'll close the prayer time in a minute or so, perhaps leaving some of them wishing they had dared to contribute. Nothing is lost. They will join into it next week!

SEVEN

Fellowship

Christian living is not an isolated affair. It means belonging with others in God's countercultural society, the church. You suggested a bring-and-share supper last week, and they will be amazed to see how it all worked out. That itself will be a mark of the fellowship that is the theme for this evening. You might ask how people are finding personal Bible reading and prayer, and if they are finding *Newness of Life* a help. If some have not started, this may prick them into action!

The Talk

Ask what image the word "church" brings to their minds! Then show them some of the New Testament descriptions of the church. It is the *Family of God* in which we are all brothers and sisters (Galatians 4:4-7; Ephesians 2:17-19). It is the *Temple of the Holy Spirit* in which we are all spiritual stones (Ephesians 2:19-22; 1Corinthians 3:16). It is a *Colony of Heaven* in which we're citizens (Philippians 3:20). It is the *Body of Christ* in which we are limbs (Ephesians 4:15,16). It is the

Army of God in which we're soldiers (Ephesians 6:10-20). Its destiny is to be the *Bride of Christ* (Ephesians 5:25-33; Revelation 21:2-8). These images are sure to provoke some discussion.

Get them to see that the church is both universal and local, and that its main functions are threefold.

Worship – *Our responsibility to God.*

Fellowship – *Our responsibility to one another.*

Witness and Service – *Our responsibility to the world that Christ died for.*

(1"Peter 2:1-12 interweaves all three functions!)

You'll need to say something about the unity of the church. Jesus prayed for his disciples to be one (John 17:20f) and they managed it, more or less, in the early centuries. In due course human frailty and insistence on particular emphases led to denominations. But God hates division in his people.

Despite all appearances, there *is* a God-given unity among all who have entrusted their lives to Christ (Ephesians 4:4-6), and we must strive to preserve and regain that unity. Among people who agree on the deity of Jesus Christ, *that he is God,* and on the reliability of the Bible, "church-craft" and worship styles at the lesser level become relatively unimportant, being matters of one's choice and taste.

The New Testament knows nothing of a clergy-laity hierarchy. (That's why the definition of *church* is the same in the Anglican Articles of Religion and the Lutheran and Calvinist confessions of faith: "The visible Church of Christ is a congregation of faithful people, in which the pure Word of God is preached, and the Sacraments are ministered as Christ has ordained." No mention of the clergy!)

And the NT knows nothing of denominations.

The church is a one-class society transcending all barriers of gender, color, education, society, and of course nationality (Ephesians 2:14-18; Galatians 3:28). The New Testament knows nothing of differing status among Christians, of differing functions (Ephesians 4:11,12). Love is the bond that should unite us all (Colossians 3:14).

At the end of this talk it would be good to talk a bit about Baptism – the once for all launch into Christianity – and also about Holy Communion, the repeated nourishment the Lord offers us along the way. Jesus left us both, being the only two sacraments he himself instituted, and they are *important.*

A helpful way of understanding the Communion is via a number of "looks." *Look back* to the cross in gratitude. *Look inwardly* with repentance for sins committed. *Look round* in love for fellow participants. *Look up* in faith for the Lord's nourishment. *Look to* the sacrament's own retelling of the old, old story of Jesus and his love for us. *Look forward* with expectancy to the heavenly banquet. And *look outwardly* with wholeheartedness to serve a needy world.

The Verse To Learn

1Corinthians 12:27 "Now you are the body of Christ, and each one of you is a part of it." Christ's body is how he expresses himself on earth today, and we are all interdependent limbs in it. This is a great verse to show normally very independent Westerners the importance of interdependence.

Take a few moments to see how well they have remembered the previous verses.

The Bible Study

Romans 12:1-13. This is a great passage touching on many aspects of Christian worship. The folks are likely to be exhilarated by it and take-off on it, but here are some useful questions, if needed:

1. What does true worship involve?
2. If the church is Christ's body on earth, what implications follow? Do you see them in your local church?
3. If "each member belongs to all the others" what does this mean for our relationships?
4. What does this say about the practical outcome of full surrender to Christ? Is anything holding you back from "presenting your body as a living sacrifice"?
5. According to St. Paul we all have different gifts and abilities. What do each of you think you have? What do others in the group think you

have? How is it being used for good in your Christian community?

The Prayer Time

Get them into pairs for this. Have them pray for the discernment and the use of each other's gifts. Then say "Think of one thing you would love to see happen in your church. Pray for it now and daily in the coming week." Or if some haven't a church, "Ask God to show you to the church that's right for you, one where you will be able to serve him. Pray about that now and daily in the coming week."

The Review

Check-up on the pastoral side. Have we all had at least one session with those allotted to us? Then for a little relaxation, share news of how each other's Bible study and prayer time is going.

EIGHT

The Holy Spirit

This is the group's penultimate evening, and it often provides a spur to any who have not yet invited the Spirit into their lives. The Holy Spirit is the life of God in the world of men. He was active at the creation of the world (Genesis 1:2f; 2:7). In the Old Testament we find him primarily inspiring the prophets but also empowering particular individuals like kings and judges for special tasks. The Old Testament looked for the arrival of the Messiah when the Spirit would be widely available (Ezekiel 36:25-27; Jeremiah 31:31-34). Jesus the Messiah was uniquely filled with the Holy Spirit (John 1:32ff;7:37-39). He promised that after his death the Spirit, his "other self," would come and live in believers (John 14:15-18;16:7-15). That is exactly what happened at Pentecost. Now, in contrast to Old Testament days, the Spirit is for all believers, not just some. He is not fitful but remains with us forever, and the Spirit is no loner impersonal, but marked with the personal imprint of Jesus.

Some of this background may be important to share with them. Choose from this background information those things you are led to believe they'll need to hear this evening.

The Talk

There are at least three things about the Holy Spirit that new Christians need to be aware of.

The Fruit of the Spirit

The Holy Spirit enters our lives at the time of our conversion (Galatians 4:6). He then sets to work getting lovely fruit to grow in the garden of our lives. Show them Galatians 5:22-24. As the branches stay attached in the vine, the sap of God's Spirit slowly but surely produces fruit (John 15:1-15). *We ourselves* cannot create these fruits of character. But *we* certainly can prevent them, if we grieve or quench the Holy Spirit (Ephesians 4:30; 1Thessalonians 5:19). If we've done that it calls for repentance and restoration.

The Gifts of the Spirit

The Holy Spirit is a great giver. He gave inspiration to the scriptures (2Peter 1:21), new life to people like us (John 3:5) and he longs to equip us with other gifts. Some of them are seen in 1Corinthians 12:4ff and 27ff. These gifts are not for our gratification; they are for building up the Christian community.

The Holy Spirit's supreme aim is to make us like Christ (2Corinthians 3:18).

The Power of the Spirit

Temptation is a universal thing we all experience, and it *increases* not decreases after we have become Christians – because we have changed sides, of course. Temptation comes through *"the world"* (society, which leaves God out, 1John 2:15,16); *"the flesh"* (our own fallen nature (Romans 7:21-23), and '"the devil" (the anti-God force of evil (1Thessalonians 3:5).

The way to overcome temptation is by claiming the Lord's mighty power as soon as temptation strikes (1Corinthians 10:13).

Things they need to remember include:

1. Temptation is not sin, but yielding to it is.

2. Jesus was tempted more than any of us, and never gave in (Hebrews 4:15). He is the champion.

3. Because Jesus won the war with the devil he can win our battles too (Hebrews 2:18).

4. There is always a way of escape that God provides – *if* we will take it (1Corinthians 10:13).

5. We can lose a lot of battles and still win the war. Because He does not give up on us (1John 2:2f).

Here are things they need to avoid:

1. Don't *"flirt with the world"* in terms of its society, worldly films, magazines, the

pornographic web, or worldly ambitions that could dull their love for Christ.

2. Don't *"spare the flesh."* Don't go easy on the old pre-Christian selfish (it's all about me!) nature. It needs daily to be put back on the cross so that the Holy Spirit can preside in our lives and shine through us (Galatians 2:20).

3. Don't *"compromise with the devil."* Resist him! (James 4:7; 1Peter 5:9), and keep well clear of the occult (Acts19:18-20). That means things as seemingly harmless as the daily astrology report in a newspaper.

A half-hearted Christian life is a miserable life!

The Verse To Learn

Philippians 4:13 "I can do all things through Christ who strengthens me." If I should think *"Well, I can cope,"* that would be arrogant (and foolish). But to think "I just can't cope" would spell despair, wouldn't it? But when we realise our weakness, and claim Christ's strength, then we are up for anything.

The Bible Study

1Corinthians 12:1-13. You may need to tell them the background of this passage. Members of this young, gifted church were flashing their spiritual gifts around, and Paul is seeking to bind them into a partnership.

Questions, if you need them, might include:

1. How does verse 3 link Jesus and the Holy Spirit?
2. What do you learn from the variety of gifts and their unified source?

3. What do verses 8-10 teach us about the kinds of ministries we should be exercising in our own churches?

4. What is meant by "being given one Spirit to drink"? (See John 7:37-39)

5. Does this passage give any support to the idea that there are two kinds of Christians, ordinary or "Spirit-filled"?

6. Are you willing to ask the Holy Spirit to fill you, develop your character, and give you whatever gifts are needed for the work he calls you to do?

The Prayer Time

If any of them know that they have not yet invited the Holy Spirit into their lives, this might be a splendid opportunity to ask Him to come in. More generally, you should encourage them to pray for each other's future growth as Christians after the course is over, and for the power of the Holy Spirit in their lives. There is plenty in the passage itself to prompt praise and prayer.

The Review

Realising that next week is the final session, get a report from fellow leaders on where the members of the group stand, and what plans are already in place for the next step in their Christian lives. There may be introductions to be made in the new world of Christian fellowship, suggestions to be offered. You may want to do something special on the last night, like giving them each a New Testament. Anything like this needs to be thought of in advance.

NINE

Witness And Service

This last evening together will probably have a lot of warmth and some nostalgia. The aim is to help them be ready to move on in the Christian life and to look outwards to a needy world. Hence tonight's theme of Witness and Service.

The Talk

Witness

We don't join a sports team or the army or police, without being willing to put on the uniform. We want to make it crystal clear we belong. And it is the same with the Christian life. Jesus told his followers that if they were not prepared to confess him before men, then he would not be able to confess them before his Father in heaven (Matthew 10:32). Some people are ashamed to admit they are Christians, or they'll soft-pedal their allegiance if they are in the company of non-believers. Some keep a low profile, hoping nobody will ask! But we are called to be unashamed about our love for Christ. Romans 10:9,10 makes it crystal clear that public confession of Christ is the counterpart to private commitment to him. It is only if we "believe in our heart and confess with our mouth" that we shall be saved. *Secret disciples are a liability to the Christian cause!*

In places like Indonesia and many others Christians risk getting killed simply for belonging to Christ, yet in the West we hardly dare mention the name of Christ outside of a church service! The Lord calls us to something better than this. The New Testament insists that we all are called to be witnesses to Jesus. Not preachers, although that is the calling of some. But all are called to be *witnesses.* A witness must be able to relate "I have found this to be true in my own experience," and nobody can argue against that. See Acts 2:32. Only Peter was preaching on that occasion, but all of the apostles were bearing witness. We need fewer indifferent preachers and many more confident witnesses! Like St. Paul, every believer can say "I am not ashamed of the gospel, for it is the power of God for the salvation of everyone who believes" (Romans 1:16).

After all, how can people know the reality of Jesus unless those who know him are prepared to say so?

Service

Every Christian is by definition a *minister* of Christ. Do not restrict the use of the word minister to pastors and missionaries.

You cannot be a Christian without being a *minister*! There are three main words for minister or servant in the New Testament, and all three are applied to every Christian.

The first of these words means *slave* (1Peter 2:16; Revelation 1:1) and describes the total surrender of every part of our lives – home, work, ambitions, the lot of it – to Jesus, who sacrificed everything for us. A new Christian could profitably ponder Romans 12:2 and 1Corinthians 6:19,20. We do not belong to ourselves. We have been bought at a great price. We are called therefore to glorify God in our bodily behaviour. In ancient society a slave had no rights, but was totally at the command of his or her master. The New Testament writers deliberately and provocatively chose this word *slave* to describe their relation to Jesus. Would the group now feel able to describe their dedication to Christ in this way?

The second New Testament word for minister means *worship leader*. It is the word from which we get the word *liturgy*. It speaks of our worship (Acts 13:2). Worship is a big word. It means celebrating the *worth* of the Lord we love. It includes our *giving* (2Corinthians 9:12), our *faith* (Philippians 2:17), *doing* our job well (Romans 13.6), and even *telling* others about Christ (Romans 15:16). You can encourage the group to ask themselves how important worship in this broader sense has become to them (versus just an hour on Sunday)? What does it cost them? Has it spilled over yet into telling others about the Lord?

If not, their Christian life will, sadly, grow stale.

The third NT word for servant or one who renders a service means *helper.* Our word *deacon* is derived from it. It is widely used in the Bible for practical help of all kinds. It describes our own relationship to those who are fellow Christians and to those who, as yet, are not. Prison visiting and personal service (Philemon 13; Acts 19:22), handing out soup and preaching are all called by this word *service* (Acts 6:1-4). Since the coming of Jesus into the world we must no longer insulate the sacred from the secular. "This is how one should regard us, as servants of Christ" said the apostle. (1Corinthians 4:1)

The group leader could encourage the members to reflect on what changes becoming a Christian has brought into their lives the areas of wholeheartedness, worship, and practical service.

After completing the talk I say something like this, "We have been thinking about opening our mouths and giving witness to Jesus, haven't we? Right, let's do it. You have a very friendly and affirming group here. Tell us if you have come to Christ yet, and if so what difference he is making to you." It may seem risky, but it works, and I find they will all give some sort of witness, knowing it's the end of the course. It always leads to considerable rejoicing and encouragement all round.

The Verse To Learn

Romans 12:1 "In view of God's mercies, offer your bodies as a living sacrifice, holy and pleasing to God –

this is your spiritual act of worship." It's a bit long to learn, but it admirably summarises the night's theme.

The Bible Study

Acts 5:40-6:8. This is a rich passage about different types of service among the early church, and should stimulate ideas for members of the group. Some useful questions might include the following:

1. What motivated these people to want to serve the Lord? What motivates you?
2. What was it the disciples "multiplied" in Jerusalem?
3. What service are you now engaged in that you would not be if you were not a Christian?
4. What new area of fellowship and service is each of you going to commit yourself to now that this Short Course has ended? Be specific.

The Prayer Time

Prayer should flow very readily by now. Encourage people to thank God for the difference he is making in their lives, and then to pray by name for each other and for one other person they want to find Christ.

You will have taken special note of the situation in each member's life, and what the next step or steps appear to be for them. You will have ensured that each person has had at least a couple of personal chats with one of the leadership team, and that all of them have a

Bible and *Newness of Life* notes. You will have referred or connected each of them to the pastor of a church of their choice (or if not you will do it in the next day or two.) Thus before they go you have made sure that each has a church to attend, a small group to join, and a suitable next step to look forward to. This means you leaders will have had to spend some real time and energy gathering your understanding of where each of them is in their walk and, as needed, assisting them in making suitable arrangements. And make it plain that you are available for them to come to at any time in the future if it would help them.

End with some sort of special food and drink to celebrate! After they have all left, you'll have the final debrief with your colleagues.

The Review

You thank your leaders with all your heart for their dedicated work over the past six weeks.

The initial nurturing of the group is over.

It is the beginning of the rest of their Christian lives.

Supplement 1

Leading An Inductive Bible Study

The most important thing to remember in leading a short Bible study with new believers is that this is not a talk or series of talks with you imparting wisdom. Instead it is exposing people to scripture so that they begin to find things in it, get excited with it, and form the habit of feeding on it. You are there to facilitate this progress. There are a dozen things you should mind!

1. Ensure that they all have the same Bible with the same translation and page numbers, and you are sitting so that you can see everyone's face.

2. Either give them a page to turn to, or begin to explain the shape of the Bible like this, "The New Testament is the second half of the Bible. First there are the four Gospels, then the Acts of the Apostles, and then Romans. If you are in Acts you have not gone far enough. If you have hit the Corinthian letters you have gone too far." Too simple for some maybe, but it will be a lifeline to the embarrassed and ignorant.

3. Make sure they all have time to find the passage. Then suggest you read round in a circle, a verse at a time. This gets people used to the sound of their own voice reading the Bible, and helps to break the sound barrier that might otherwise ensue. You may need to give a few sentences explaining what the passage is about, but keep it *really* short.

4. Then give them time to read it again quietly to themselves and choose something that strikes them such as a challenge, a command, a promise, or encouragement, something they have never seen before. Tell them they will all be asked to share their discoveries with the group, after two minutes by your watch! This marvellously concentrates the mind!

5. When the two minutes are up, then invite contributions. "Who would like to start?" Someone always will! Make them say what verse they've got so that everyone can look at it.

6. Try to get them to ask themselves "What does it mean?" Then, "How does this apply to our lives?" You will find that mistakes are made in both. If what they say is wildly astray from the actual meaning of the text you may like to ask, "Okay, but what do others think it means?" and then major on the best contribution. If it is unapplied, you can bridge to that, "Great. So what is that going to mean in real life for us?"

7. Some one is sure to moan that they had wanted to choose the very verse someone else has just commented on! Say "Hey, not to worry. This book is inexhaustible. But what was it that *you* liked about this verse?"

8. You will be sure to have the professional talker in the group, who loves to speak even when they have nothing to say! Welcome their first and maybe even their second contribution, but then shut them up gently. "Hang on a moment, Robert. You've given us a couple of very helpful insights. What have you other people found?"

9. You may well have someone who loves to delve into some irrelevant side issue. Enquire gently, "Which verse did you find that in, Kathy?" Keep their noses in the text! If they come up with some major issue like predestination or suffering, it would be wise rather than involving everyone in what is a difficult and perhaps fruitless topic (which is no way the major thrust of the evening) to suggest they chat with you about it afterwards.

10. You are likely to have one or two silent people. It is best not to frighten them by asking them for a contribution, at any rate for the first couple of weeks. The third week you could! But in general, when you are about to close, say "Maybe there is someone who hasn't said anything yet this evening, who would like to contribute at this time?"

11. You will find at times that it all falls silent. So then you need to be the one to ask questions. But be specific. "There are good things in verse six here. Anyone got any ideas about it?" When asking questions make sure they can't be answered by a straight Yes or No. Questions like "Why does…?" "How do you think…?" "What does it mean…?" usually produce good reflection and answers.

12. And remember you have another resource: the questions I've suggested as appropriate for the evening's topic. It may be wise to have them unobtrusively available, for use in time of need!

When time is up, a few minutes before the advertised closing time, you might say something like this on the first evening. "We have been talking about God all evening, and he has been here among us. Let's talk to him now in our own words. Just take the thought that has helped you most tonight and turn it into a prayer or a thank-you in your own words. Don't feel embarrassed. Christians do pray out loud and God is not in the least fussy about correct grammar! So let's just haul off and go for it." I will begin and my colleague will close in a minute or two. So do chip in before that if you would like. Some will, but certainly not on all of them the first night. Do not press them. It will grow on them. You may like to suggest that they read out a bit of text they like and then pray very shortly "Thank you for that, Lord" or "Please make this true of me." Make sure your own opening prayer is a proper model – short, warm, based on the text. Others will probably take the hint.

Attention to detail is important. The nibbles need to be of good quality, the coffee hot! Welcome at the door is *very* important. I have known people to walk up and down the street before summoning the courage to come in for the first time to a house where a meeting like this is to take place!

If you are leading the evening, *always* ensure that you are sitting where you can make eye contact with everyone else in the group. (It will help you no end to be able to grasp all their reactions!) It is good practice to announce at the start of the evening the time when you will be closing each week, so people know where they stand. *Then stick to that timing!*

At the end, the room needs to be put to rights and cups and plates washed up. Leaders will be the last to leave, and will need to stay on for a short debrief on how the evening went, and for planning the next meeting.

Pastoral Care

Each leader will have two or three members of the group assigned to them for pastoral care. Before the course ends they will seek to have two unhurried private sessions with each person at a mutually convenient time. It is not a bad idea to invite your 'customer' to a meal in your home or apartment or a restaurant. This helps to make them feel a bit special. We shall have more to say about this in a later chapter, but during the first such time together you will want to establish where they stands spiritually. Have they entrusted themselves to Christ or are they still unclear about it? If they are just not there yet, you will seek to discern what the difficulty is and help them to lay hold of Christ.

If your person is clear on their commitment to Christ, it would be good to show them a verse that offers a splendid ground for assurance, 1John 5:12 for example, because the enemy would like to steal that commitment away or at least cause your new Christian to tend to question it. You will also want to begin to establish their pattern for regular Bible reading and prayer. I have found *Newness of Life* (available from *tenofthose.com*) by far the best introduction to getting a habit of regular Bible reading going. It is "undated," so can be started at any time. It contains a short passage of the Bible for each day, helpful comment on it, a thought for the day, and a prayer to use. It goes for 30 days, and takes the reader through some of the most helpful and thrilling parts of the Bible. It is certainly enough to start a lifelong habit.

The second pastoral session with your 'customer' will depend on how things have been going. Are they now clear that they have come to Christ? Have they *told* anyone? Telling others that one has become a Christian is a vitally important step to lock-in one's conversion and has eternal consequences (Matthew 10:32). Is he or she clear that it all depends on Christ's grace and not their own achievements? You may not manage to have your second session until the course is almost over, so you will want to go even further than this and discuss with your charge their next steps. What Christian group is going to be most helpful for

Your Second Session

The second session with the member of the group you are responsible for may be much shorter and it will certainly vary considerably, according to what they want to bring up. But on the whole you will want to see if they have got some good Christian friends among their peers. If not, you may be able to introduce one or two into their life. Try to ensure that they are having a regular devotional time, and are linked up with a lively church. And leave them in no doubt they can come back to you at any time in the future when they feel you could help them. Be sure to give them a business card or write out your contact information.

Supplement 3

A Pattern For The Daily Quiet Time

All Christians have discovered that it is essential for healthy spiritual life to maintain a regular time with God every day, centring on prayer and Bible reading. In prayer we speak to him. In scripture he speaks to us. Here are some simple suggestions you may like to pass on to a new Christian.

Turn to God

Find a quiet place where you can be alone with God. Many people find the beginning of the day is best, before all its pressures crowd in. Try to set aside distractions, and focus your attention on God. Think of him as he really is, the Friend who sticks closer than a brother and loves you very much. Have your Bible with you and also some helpful explanatory notes such as *Day by Day* or a similar product from the Scripture Union or from Bible Reading Fellowship. If you are using *Newness of Life* (*10ofthose.com*) for your first thirty days, you will find that it is undated, so you can start when you are ready. It also gives the text of the Bible passage, some helpful comment, a thought for the day, and a prayer to use, all on the same double page. This furnishes a brief and an encouraging introduction to regular Bible reading.

Turn to the Bible

Check the date from your Bible reading notes, and open the Bible at today's passage. Read it twice, first to get the thrust of it, and then to start looking in greater depth. Do not turn straight to the Notes (embodying other people's thoughts) or you may well discover nothing else in the passage! Turn, rather, to the text itself.

Here are some useful questions to ask yourself:

Is there something new here about God?

What does it show me about human nature?

Is there an example to follow – or avoid?

Is there a command to obey? A warning to heed?

Is there a promise to claim or a prayer I can use?

Is there a verse I want to learn by heart?

How can I apply some of this to my daily life?

What one thought will I take with me today?

Turn To Your Bible Reading Notes

See what they may add to your own discoveries.

Turn to Prayer

Many people have found the acrostic **ACTS** a helpful guide to the different aspects of prayer: **A**doration, **C**onfession, **T**hanksgiving and **S**upplication. The Lord's Prayer is not just a prayer but a marvellous pattern for prayer – as we revel in God's fatherly care, pray for his kingly rule to be extended into the lives of our friends, pray for his will to be done in our own lives, and so on.

At all events, talk to the Lord in your own words. Some find they concentrate better if they pray aloud. Some like to start off with reading a psalm. Others like to sing a chorus or hymn to the Lord before they turn to their requests. But then transpose the thoughts from today's Bible reading into prayer and thanksgiving. Then pray about other matters: the needs of your friends, your family, your work mates, your church and perhaps about the world and its needs. Look out for answers to previous prayers, and turn them into praise.

Finally commit the day to his care and guidance.

Wandering thoughts

Many people get worried at their short attention span. Part of the answer is to have only a short time with God to begin with. Another part of the answer is to turn the wandering thoughts into a short prayer. So if I am sitting near the widow and find myself over-occupied with the birds outside, just thank God for their beauty and agility and return to your previous concerns. If there are things you want to remember to do – and these often surface during a quiet time with God – jot them down on a piece of paper for action later. That preserves them but gets them out of the way of your quiet time.

The shape of our devotional times will change a good deal over our lives, but what is offered above is a simple initial approach that many will find they can manage.

About the Author

The Rev. Canon Dr. Michael Green is an Oxford theologian, Anglican Priest, Christian apologist, and the author of more than fifty Christian books. As a teacher and speaker in demand by many Christian denominations he has rightly been called a "World Asset." Notice that there is no mention in *The Way Forward* of the Anglican Church or any other church. It is Michael's gift to Christendom. Michael Green has studied at several universities, including Oxford and Cambridge, and was admitted to the degree of Doctor of Divinity by the Archbishop of Canterbury and by the University of Toronto. He has served as a curate, a parish rector, the Principal of St. Johns College, Oxford University, Chaplain of the Oxford Pastorate, Preacher at Coventry Cathedral (where is an Honorary Canon), and Tutor at the London College of Divinity. He was Professor of Evangelism at Regent College, Vancouver, from 1987 until 1992. Returning to England he became Advisor to the 103rd Archbishop of Canterbury (George Carey) and the Archbishop of York. Despite having officially retired in 1996, he became a Senior Research Fellow and Head of Evangelism and Apologetics at Wycliffe Hall, Oxford in 1997. He lives in the village of Marston, near Oxford, and is married to Rosemary. They have four adult children.

Michael Green has been a prolific writer, with much of his work written for a popular reading audience, although he has also contributed to academic studies. Many of his best known books discuss the topics of evangelism and apologetics.

One of Michael Green's objectives has been to equip lay Christian believers in their grasp of the gospel message, and to give them the confidence to converse with others on faith matters. These practical objectives are very clear in books such as *Evangelism, Now And Then* and *Sharing Your Faith With Friends And Family.* He has built on these foundational studies in his advocacy of evangelism at a parish church level, both through his personal ministry and in his book *Evangelism Through the Local Church.*

Other books by Michael Green that are currently available from *Amazon.com* include:

Thirty Years That Changed The World – The Book Of Acts For Today

Evangelism In The Early Church

"But Don't All Religions Lead To God?"

I Believe In The Holy Spirit

Arresting Grace

Who Is This Jesus?